50 Premium Steak Dinner Recipes for Home

By: Kelly Johnson

Table of Contents

- Steak au Poivre
- Herb-Crusted Ribeye with Potato Gratin
- Steak with Honey-Mustard Glaze
- Chimichurri Flank Steak with Quinoa Salad
- Garlic Butter Steak Bites
- Steak and Potato Skewers
- Grilled Hanger Steak with Pesto
- Spicy Steak Stir-Fry
- Herb-Butter Basted Steak
- Steak with Sautéed Mushrooms and Onions
- Grilled Vegetable and Steak Sandwich
- Honey Garlic Flank Steak
- Smoked Steak with Chimichurri
- Sesame-Crusted Steak with Soy Glaze
- Red Wine-Braised Beef Short Ribs
- Steak Salad with Avocado and Feta
- Mexican Street Corn and Steak Bowl
- Garlic Herb Butter Steak Sandwich
- Classic Steak and Kidney Pie
- Steak Pizzaiola

Filet Mignon with Red Wine Reduction

Ingredients:

- 2 filet mignon steaks (6-8 oz each)
- Salt and pepper to taste
- 2 tbsp olive oil
- 1 cup red wine (Cabernet Sauvignon or Merlot)
- 1/2 cup beef broth
- 2 tbsp unsalted butter
- Fresh thyme for garnish

Instructions:

1. Season Steaks: Pat the filet mignon steaks dry with paper towels. Season generously with salt and pepper.
2. Sear Steaks: In a skillet over medium-high heat, heat olive oil. Add the steaks and sear for about 3-4 minutes per side for medium-rare. Remove from skillet and let rest.
3. Make Reduction: In the same skillet, pour in the red wine and scrape the browned bits from the bottom. Bring to a boil, then reduce heat and simmer until reduced by half. Add beef broth and continue to simmer until thickened.
4. Finish Sauce: Whisk in the butter until melted and the sauce is glossy. Season with salt and pepper to taste.
5. Serve: Slice the filet mignon and drizzle the red wine reduction over the top. Garnish with fresh thyme.

Ribeye Steak with Garlic Butter

Ingredients:

- 2 ribeye steaks (8-10 oz each)
- Salt and pepper to taste
- 2 tbsp olive oil
- 1/4 cup unsalted butter, softened
- 3 cloves garlic, minced
- 1 tbsp fresh parsley, chopped

Instructions:

1. Prepare Garlic Butter: In a bowl, mix softened butter, minced garlic, and chopped parsley. Set aside.
2. Season Steaks: Season ribeye steaks generously with salt and pepper.
3. Cook Steaks: Heat olive oil in a skillet over medium-high heat. Add the steaks and cook for 5-7 minutes on each side for medium-rare, adjusting time as necessary for thickness.
4. Add Garlic Butter: During the last minute of cooking, top each steak with a spoonful of garlic butter, allowing it to melt over the steaks.
5. Serve: Let the steaks rest for a few minutes before slicing. Serve with additional garlic butter on top.

New York Strip with Herb Compound Butter

Ingredients:

- 2 New York strip steaks (8-10 oz each)
- Salt and pepper to taste
- 2 tbsp olive oil
- 1/4 cup unsalted butter, softened
- 1 tbsp fresh chives, chopped
- 1 tbsp fresh parsley, chopped
- 1 tsp fresh thyme, chopped

Instructions:

1. Prepare Compound Butter: In a bowl, combine softened butter with chives, parsley, thyme, salt, and pepper. Mix well and refrigerate until firm.
2. Season Steaks: Season New York strip steaks with salt and pepper.
3. Cook Steaks: Heat olive oil in a skillet over medium-high heat. Cook steaks for about 4-5 minutes per side for medium-rare.
4. Add Butter: During the last minute of cooking, place a slice of herb compound butter on top of each steak.
5. Serve: Let the steaks rest for a few minutes, then serve with the melted herb butter.

Grilled T-Bone Steak with Chimichurri

Ingredients:

- 2 T-bone steaks (8-10 oz each)
- Salt and pepper to taste
- 2 tbsp olive oil
- 1 cup fresh parsley, chopped
- 1/4 cup olive oil (for chimichurri)
- 2 tbsp red wine vinegar
- 2 cloves garlic, minced
- 1/2 tsp red pepper flakes
- Salt and pepper to taste

Instructions:

1. Prepare Chimichurri: In a bowl, mix parsley, olive oil, red wine vinegar, garlic, red pepper flakes, salt, and pepper. Set aside.
2. Season Steaks: Preheat the grill and season T-bone steaks with salt and pepper.
3. Grill Steaks: Grill steaks for about 5-6 minutes on each side for medium-rare, adjusting time for thickness.
4. Serve: Remove from grill and let rest. Serve with chimichurri drizzled over the top.

Porterhouse Steak with Balsamic Glaze

Ingredients:

- 2 porterhouse steaks (8-12 oz each)
- Salt and pepper to taste
- 2 tbsp olive oil
- 1/2 cup balsamic vinegar
- 2 tbsp honey
- 1 tbsp Dijon mustard

Instructions:

1. Prepare Glaze: In a saucepan, combine balsamic vinegar, honey, and Dijon mustard. Simmer over medium heat until reduced by half and thickened.
2. Season Steaks: Season porterhouse steaks with salt and pepper.
3. Cook Steaks: Heat olive oil in a skillet over medium-high heat. Add the steaks and cook for about 5-7 minutes on each side for medium-rare.
4. Drizzle Glaze: Drizzle the balsamic glaze over the steaks before serving.

Steak Frites with Béarnaise Sauce

Ingredients:

- 2 sirloin steaks (8-10 oz each)
- Salt and pepper to taste
- 2 tbsp olive oil
- 1 lb frozen French fries
- 1/2 cup unsalted butter
- 2 egg yolks
- 1 tbsp white wine vinegar
- 1 tbsp fresh tarragon, chopped
- Salt and pepper to taste

Instructions:

1. Cook Fries: Bake or fry French fries according to package instructions.
2. Prepare Béarnaise Sauce: In a saucepan, melt butter. In a separate bowl, whisk egg yolks and vinegar until pale and thick. Gradually add melted butter while whisking. Stir in tarragon, salt, and pepper.
3. Season Steaks: Season sirloin steaks with salt and pepper.
4. Cook Steaks: Heat olive oil in a skillet over medium-high heat. Cook steaks for about 4-5 minutes on each side for medium-rare.
5. Serve: Serve steaks with French fries and Béarnaise sauce on the side.

Beef Wellington

Ingredients:

- 2 lb beef tenderloin
- Salt and pepper to taste
- 2 tbsp olive oil
- 8 oz mushrooms, finely chopped
- 1 onion, chopped
- 2 cloves garlic, minced
- 4 oz pâté (optional)
- 1 sheet puff pastry
- 1 egg, beaten

Instructions:

1. Sear Beef: Season beef tenderloin with salt and pepper. Heat olive oil in a skillet over high heat and sear the beef on all sides until browned. Remove and let cool.
2. Prepare Mushroom Duxelles: In the same skillet, add mushrooms, onion, and garlic. Cook until moisture is evaporated and mixture is dry. Let cool.
3. Assemble Wellington: Roll out puff pastry. Spread pâté on pastry (if using), then add mushroom mixture, followed by the beef. Wrap the pastry around the beef, sealing the edges.
4. Bake: Preheat oven to 400°F (200°C). Brush the pastry with beaten egg. Bake for 25-30 minutes until golden brown. Let rest for 10 minutes before slicing.
5. Serve: Slice and serve warm.

Sirloin Steak with Blue Cheese Crust

Ingredients:

- 2 sirloin steaks (8 oz each)
- Salt and pepper to taste
- 1 tbsp olive oil
- 1/2 cup blue cheese, crumbled
- 1/4 cup breadcrumbs
- 2 tbsp fresh parsley, chopped
- 1 tbsp Dijon mustard

Instructions:

1. Preheat Oven: Preheat your oven to 400°F (200°C).
2. Prepare Blue Cheese Mixture: In a bowl, combine crumbled blue cheese, breadcrumbs, parsley, and mustard. Mix well.
3. Season Steaks: Season sirloin steaks with salt and pepper. Heat olive oil in an oven-safe skillet over medium-high heat. Sear steaks for 3-4 minutes on each side until browned.
4. Add Topping: Remove from heat and spread the blue cheese mixture evenly on top of each steak.
5. Bake: Transfer the skillet to the oven and bake for 5-7 minutes for medium-rare or until desired doneness.
6. Serve: Let rest for a few minutes before slicing and serving.

Flank Steak Tacos with Avocado Salsa

Ingredients:

- 1 lb flank steak
- Salt and pepper to taste
- 2 tbsp olive oil
- 8 corn tortillas
- 1 avocado, diced
- 1/2 cup diced tomatoes
- 1/4 cup red onion, chopped
- 1 lime, juiced
- Cilantro for garnish

Instructions:

1. Season and Cook Steak: Season flank steak with salt and pepper. Heat olive oil in a skillet over medium-high heat. Cook steak for about 4-5 minutes per side until medium-rare. Remove and let rest.
2. Make Avocado Salsa: In a bowl, combine diced avocado, tomatoes, red onion, lime juice, salt, and pepper.
3. Slice Steak: Slice the flank steak against the grain into thin strips.
4. Assemble Tacos: Warm corn tortillas. Top each tortilla with steak slices and avocado salsa.
5. Serve: Garnish with cilantro and serve immediately.

Coffee-Crusted Steak with Maple Glaze

Ingredients:

- 2 steaks (ribeye or sirloin)
- 2 tbsp coffee grounds
- Salt and pepper to taste
- 1 tbsp olive oil
- 1/4 cup maple syrup
- 1 tbsp balsamic vinegar

Instructions:

1. Prepare Coffee Rub: In a small bowl, mix coffee grounds, salt, and pepper. Rub this mixture onto both sides of the steaks.
2. Cook Steaks: Heat olive oil in a skillet over medium-high heat. Cook steaks for about 4-5 minutes per side for medium-rare.
3. Make Maple Glaze: In a small saucepan, combine maple syrup and balsamic vinegar. Simmer until slightly thickened.
4. Serve: Drizzle the maple glaze over the cooked steaks and serve warm.

Grilled Sirloin with Roasted Vegetables

Ingredients:

- 2 sirloin steaks (8 oz each)
- Salt and pepper to taste
- 2 tbsp olive oil
- 1 zucchini, sliced
- 1 bell pepper, chopped
- 1 red onion, chopped
- 1 tsp Italian seasoning

Instructions:

1. Preheat Oven: Preheat your oven to 425°F (220°C).
2. Prepare Vegetables: Toss zucchini, bell pepper, and onion with olive oil, Italian seasoning, salt, and pepper. Spread on a baking sheet and roast for 20-25 minutes.
3. Season and Grill Steaks: Season sirloin steaks with salt and pepper. Heat a grill pan over medium-high heat and grill steaks for 4-5 minutes per side for medium-rare.
4. Serve: Serve the grilled steaks alongside the roasted vegetables.

Asian Marinated Skirt Steak

Ingredients:

- 1 lb skirt steak
- 1/4 cup soy sauce
- 2 tbsp rice vinegar
- 1 tbsp sesame oil
- 2 cloves garlic, minced
- 1 tbsp ginger, grated
- 2 green onions, chopped

Instructions:

1. Prepare Marinade: In a bowl, mix soy sauce, rice vinegar, sesame oil, garlic, and ginger.
2. Marinate Steak: Place skirt steak in a resealable bag and pour the marinade over it. Seal and refrigerate for at least 30 minutes, preferably 2 hours.
3. Cook Steak: Remove from marinade and grill or pan-sear for 3-4 minutes on each side for medium-rare.
4. Serve: Slice against the grain and garnish with chopped green onions.

Steak and Mushroom Stroganoff

Ingredients:

- 1 lb beef sirloin, cut into strips
- Salt and pepper to taste
- 2 tbsp olive oil
- 8 oz mushrooms, sliced
- 1 onion, chopped
- 2 cloves garlic, minced
- 1 cup beef broth
- 1 cup sour cream
- 1 tbsp flour
- Fresh parsley for garnish

Instructions:

1. Cook Beef: In a skillet, heat olive oil over medium-high heat. Season beef strips with salt and pepper, then cook until browned. Remove and set aside.
2. Sauté Vegetables: In the same skillet, add onions and garlic, cooking until softened. Add mushrooms and cook until browned.
3. Make Sauce: Sprinkle flour over the vegetables, stir, then slowly add beef broth. Bring to a simmer and cook until slightly thickened.
4. Finish Stroganoff: Stir in sour cream and return the beef to the skillet. Heat through and adjust seasoning.
5. Serve: Serve over egg noodles or rice, garnished with parsley.

Cajun Ribeye with Spicy Remoulade

Ingredients:

- 2 ribeye steaks (8-10 oz each)
- 2 tbsp Cajun seasoning
- Salt and pepper to taste
- 1/4 cup mayonnaise
- 1 tbsp Dijon mustard
- 1 tbsp hot sauce
- 1 tbsp capers, chopped
- 1 tbsp fresh parsley, chopped

Instructions:

1. Season Steaks: Rub Cajun seasoning over ribeye steaks. Season with additional salt and pepper if desired.
2. Cook Steaks: Heat a skillet or grill over medium-high heat. Cook steaks for 5-7 minutes per side for medium-rare.
3. Make Remoulade: In a bowl, mix mayonnaise, Dijon mustard, hot sauce, capers, and parsley.
4. Serve: Serve the ribeye steaks with a side of spicy remoulade for dipping.

Braised Short Ribs with Red Wine Sauce

Ingredients:

- 4 lbs beef short ribs
- Salt and pepper to taste
- 2 tbsp olive oil
- 1 onion, chopped
- 2 carrots, chopped
- 2 celery stalks, chopped
- 4 cloves garlic, minced
- 1 cup red wine
- 2 cups beef broth
- 2 sprigs thyme
- 1 bay leaf

Instructions:

1. Preheat Oven: Preheat your oven to 325°F (160°C).
2. Season and Brown Ribs: Season short ribs with salt and pepper. In a large Dutch oven, heat olive oil over medium-high heat. Brown the ribs on all sides, then remove and set aside.
3. Sauté Vegetables: In the same pot, add onion, carrots, and celery. Sauté until softened, about 5-7 minutes. Add garlic and cook for an additional minute.
4. Deglaze with Wine: Pour in red wine and scrape up any browned bits. Bring to a simmer and cook for 5 minutes.
5. Add Broth and Herbs: Return the short ribs to the pot. Add beef broth, thyme, and bay leaf. Bring to a boil.
6. Braise: Cover and transfer to the oven. Braise for 2.5-3 hours until the meat is tender.
7. Serve: Remove the ribs and strain the sauce. Serve the ribs with the red wine sauce drizzled over them.

Steak Salad with Balsamic Vinaigrette

Ingredients:

- 2 sirloin steaks (8 oz each)
- Salt and pepper to taste
- 6 cups mixed salad greens
- 1 cup cherry tomatoes, halved
- 1/2 red onion, thinly sliced
- 1/2 cup feta cheese, crumbled
- 1/4 cup balsamic vinegar
- 1/4 cup olive oil
- 1 tsp Dijon mustard

Instructions:

1. Season and Cook Steaks: Season steaks with salt and pepper. Grill or pan-sear for about 4-5 minutes per side for medium-rare. Let rest, then slice thinly.
2. Make Vinaigrette: In a bowl, whisk together balsamic vinegar, olive oil, Dijon mustard, salt, and pepper.
3. Assemble Salad: In a large bowl, combine salad greens, cherry tomatoes, red onion, and feta cheese. Drizzle with vinaigrette and toss gently.
4. Serve: Top the salad with sliced steak and serve immediately.

Garlic Rosemary Grilled Steak

Ingredients:

- 2 ribeye or sirloin steaks (8 oz each)
- 3 cloves garlic, minced
- 2 tbsp fresh rosemary, chopped
- 1/4 cup olive oil
- Salt and pepper to taste

Instructions:

1. Marinate Steaks: In a small bowl, mix minced garlic, rosemary, olive oil, salt, and pepper. Rub this mixture onto the steaks. Marinate for at least 30 minutes.
2. Preheat Grill: Preheat your grill to medium-high heat.
3. Grill Steaks: Grill steaks for about 4-5 minutes per side for medium-rare, or to your desired doneness.
4. Serve: Let the steaks rest for a few minutes before slicing and serving.

Beef Bulgogi with Rice

Ingredients:

- 1 lb flank steak, thinly sliced
- 1/4 cup soy sauce
- 2 tbsp brown sugar
- 2 tbsp sesame oil
- 2 cloves garlic, minced
- 1 tbsp ginger, grated
- 1 green onion, chopped
- Cooked rice for serving
- Sesame seeds for garnish

Instructions:

1. Make Marinade: In a bowl, combine soy sauce, brown sugar, sesame oil, garlic, ginger, and green onion. Add sliced beef and marinate for at least 30 minutes.
2. Cook Beef: Heat a skillet over medium-high heat. Cook marinated beef for 5-7 minutes until cooked through.
3. Serve: Serve the beef over cooked rice, garnished with sesame seeds.

Teriyaki Steak Skewers

Ingredients:

- 1 lb flank steak, cut into cubes
- 1/4 cup soy sauce
- 2 tbsp brown sugar
- 1 tbsp rice vinegar
- 1 tbsp sesame oil
- 1 clove garlic, minced
- Green bell pepper and onion, cut into chunks
- Skewers (if wooden, soaked in water)

Instructions:

1. Prepare Marinade: In a bowl, mix soy sauce, brown sugar, rice vinegar, sesame oil, and garlic.
2. Marinate Steak: Add steak cubes to the marinade and let sit for at least 30 minutes.
3. Assemble Skewers: Thread steak and vegetables onto skewers.
4. Grill Skewers: Preheat grill to medium-high heat. Grill skewers for 8-10 minutes, turning occasionally until desired doneness.
5. Serve: Serve with additional teriyaki sauce if desired.

Maple-Glazed Steak with Brussels Sprouts

Ingredients:

- 2 ribeye steaks (8 oz each)
- Salt and pepper to taste
- 2 tbsp maple syrup
- 1 lb Brussels sprouts, halved
- 2 tbsp olive oil

Instructions:

1. Preheat Oven: Preheat your oven to 400°F (200°C).
2. Prepare Brussels Sprouts: Toss Brussels sprouts with olive oil, salt, and pepper. Spread on a baking sheet and roast for 20-25 minutes until tender.
3. Cook Steaks: Season steaks with salt and pepper. Heat a skillet over medium-high heat and sear steaks for 4-5 minutes per side for medium-rare.
4. Add Maple Glaze: During the last minute of cooking, brush maple syrup over the steaks.
5. Serve: Serve steaks with roasted Brussels sprouts.

Greek Marinated Steak with Tzatziki

Ingredients:

- 2 sirloin steaks (8 oz each)
- 1/4 cup olive oil
- 2 tbsp red wine vinegar
- 2 cloves garlic, minced
- 1 tbsp dried oregano
- Salt and pepper to taste
- 1 cup Greek yogurt
- 1/2 cucumber, grated
- 1 clove garlic, minced
- 1 tbsp lemon juice

Instructions:

1. Marinate Steaks: In a bowl, mix olive oil, red wine vinegar, garlic, oregano, salt, and pepper. Add steaks and marinate for at least 30 minutes.
2. Make Tzatziki: In another bowl, combine Greek yogurt, grated cucumber, garlic, lemon juice, salt, and pepper. Mix well.
3. Cook Steaks: Grill or pan-sear marinated steaks for about 4-5 minutes per side for medium-rare.
4. Serve: Serve sliced steak with tzatziki sauce on the side.

Southwest Rubbed Steak with Corn Salsa

Ingredients:

- 2 ribeye steaks (8 oz each)
- 2 tbsp southwest seasoning (store-bought or homemade)
- 1 cup corn (fresh or frozen)
- 1/2 red bell pepper, diced
- 1/4 red onion, diced
- 1 lime, juiced
- 2 tbsp cilantro, chopped
- Salt and pepper to taste

Instructions:

1. Season Steaks: Rub southwest seasoning on both sides of the steaks. Let sit for 15 minutes.
2. Make Corn Salsa: In a bowl, combine corn, red bell pepper, red onion, lime juice, cilantro, salt, and pepper. Set aside.
3. Cook Steaks: Heat a grill or skillet over medium-high heat. Cook steaks for 4-5 minutes per side for medium-rare.
4. Serve: Slice steaks and top with corn salsa before serving.

Peppercorn-Crusted Steak with Cognac Sauce

Ingredients:

- 2 filet mignon steaks (6 oz each)
- 2 tbsp crushed black peppercorns
- Salt to taste
- 2 tbsp olive oil
- 1/4 cup cognac
- 1 cup heavy cream
- 1 tbsp Dijon mustard

Instructions:

1. Season Steaks: Press crushed peppercorns and salt onto both sides of the steaks.
2. Sear Steaks: Heat olive oil in a skillet over medium-high heat. Cook steaks for about 4-5 minutes per side for medium-rare. Remove and let rest.
3. Make Sauce: In the same skillet, add cognac and cook for 1-2 minutes. Stir in heavy cream and Dijon mustard. Simmer for 5 minutes.
4. Serve: Slice steaks and drizzle cognac sauce over them.

Steak and Lobster Tail

Ingredients:

- 2 ribeye steaks (8 oz each)
- 2 lobster tails
- 4 tbsp butter, melted
- 2 cloves garlic, minced
- Salt and pepper to taste
- Lemon wedges for serving

Instructions:

1. Cook Lobster Tails: Preheat oven to 350°F (175°C). Place lobster tails in a baking dish, brush with half the melted butter, and season with garlic, salt, and pepper. Bake for 12-15 minutes.
2. Cook Steaks: Season steaks with salt and pepper. Heat a grill or skillet over medium-high heat. Cook steaks for 4-5 minutes per side for medium-rare.
3. Serve: Plate steaks with lobster tails, drizzle remaining butter over the lobster, and serve with lemon wedges.

Grilled Steak with Mango Salsa

Ingredients:

- 2 flank steaks (8 oz each)
- Salt and pepper to taste
- 1 ripe mango, diced
- 1/2 red onion, diced
- 1 jalapeño, seeded and diced
- Juice of 1 lime
- 1/4 cup cilantro, chopped

Instructions:

1. Season Steaks: Season flank steaks with salt and pepper. Let sit for 15 minutes.
2. Make Mango Salsa: In a bowl, combine mango, red onion, jalapeño, lime juice, cilantro, salt, and pepper. Set aside.
3. Grill Steaks: Preheat grill to medium-high heat. Grill steaks for 4-5 minutes per side for medium-rare. Let rest before slicing.
4. Serve: Serve sliced steaks topped with mango salsa.

Steak Tacos with Chipotle Cream

Ingredients:

- 1 lb skirt steak, sliced thin
- Salt and pepper to taste
- 8 corn tortillas
- 1/2 cup sour cream
- 1-2 chipotle peppers in adobo sauce, minced
- 1 lime, juiced
- Cilantro for garnish

Instructions:

1. Cook Steak: Season steak with salt and pepper. Heat a skillet over medium-high heat and cook steak for about 3-4 minutes per side. Remove and let rest.
2. Make Chipotle Cream: In a bowl, mix sour cream, minced chipotle peppers, lime juice, and salt.
3. Assemble Tacos: Warm tortillas, fill with sliced steak, and drizzle chipotle cream on top. Garnish with cilantro.
4. Serve: Serve tacos with lime wedges on the side.

Stuffed Flank Steak with Spinach and Cheese

Ingredients:

- 1 flank steak (2 lbs)
- 2 cups fresh spinach, sautéed
- 1 cup ricotta cheese
- 1/2 cup feta cheese, crumbled
- Salt and pepper to taste
- Olive oil for searing

Instructions:

1. Prepare Filling: In a bowl, mix sautéed spinach, ricotta, feta, salt, and pepper.
2. Stuff Steak: Butterfly the flank steak by slicing it horizontally without cutting all the way through. Open it up and spread the cheese mixture over one half. Fold the other half over and secure with toothpicks or kitchen twine.
3. Sear Steak: Heat olive oil in a skillet over medium-high heat. Sear the stuffed steak for 3-4 minutes per side, then transfer to a preheated oven at 375°F (190°C) for 15-20 minutes.
4. Serve: Let rest before slicing and serve.

Grilled Steak with Garlic Mashed Potatoes

Ingredients:

- 2 sirloin steaks (8 oz each)
- Salt and pepper to taste
- 4 large potatoes, peeled and diced
- 4 cloves garlic, minced
- 1/2 cup heavy cream
- 1/4 cup butter

Instructions:

1. Cook Potatoes: Boil potatoes in salted water until tender, about 15 minutes. Drain and return to pot.
2. Make Garlic Mashed Potatoes: Add minced garlic, heavy cream, and butter to potatoes. Mash until smooth. Season with salt and pepper.
3. Cook Steaks: Season steaks with salt and pepper. Grill or pan-sear for 4-5 minutes per side for medium-rare.
4. Serve: Plate steaks with a generous serving of garlic mashed potatoes.

Lemon Herb Marinated Skirt Steak

Ingredients:

- 1 lb skirt steak
- 1/4 cup olive oil
- Juice of 2 lemons
- 3 cloves garlic, minced
- 1 tsp dried oregano
- 1 tsp dried thyme
- Salt and pepper to taste

Instructions:

1. Prepare Marinade: In a bowl, whisk together olive oil, lemon juice, garlic, oregano, thyme, salt, and pepper.
2. Marinate Steak: Place skirt steak in a resealable plastic bag or dish and pour the marinade over it. Marinate in the refrigerator for at least 1 hour (up to overnight).
3. Cook Steak: Preheat grill to medium-high heat. Remove steak from marinade and grill for 4-5 minutes per side for medium-rare.
4. Serve: Let rest for a few minutes before slicing against the grain and serving.

BBQ Steak with Grilled Vegetables

Ingredients:

- 2 ribeye steaks (8 oz each)
- Salt and pepper to taste
- 1 zucchini, sliced
- 1 red bell pepper, sliced
- 1 yellow bell pepper, sliced
- 2 tbsp olive oil
- BBQ sauce for brushing

Instructions:

1. Prep Vegetables: Toss sliced vegetables with olive oil, salt, and pepper.
2. Grill Steak and Vegetables: Preheat grill to medium-high heat. Season steaks with salt and pepper. Grill steaks for 4-5 minutes per side, brushing with BBQ sauce during the last few minutes. Grill vegetables for 4-6 minutes until tender.
3. Serve: Plate the steak alongside the grilled vegetables.

Steak au Poivre

Ingredients:

- 2 filet mignon steaks (6 oz each)
- 2 tbsp whole black peppercorns, crushed
- Salt to taste
- 2 tbsp olive oil
- 1/4 cup cognac
- 1 cup heavy cream
- 1 tbsp Dijon mustard

Instructions:

1. Season Steaks: Press crushed peppercorns and salt onto both sides of the steaks.
2. Sear Steaks: Heat olive oil in a skillet over medium-high heat. Cook steaks for 4-5 minutes per side for medium-rare. Remove and let rest.
3. Make Sauce: In the same skillet, add cognac and cook for 1-2 minutes. Stir in heavy cream and Dijon mustard, simmering for 5 minutes.
4. Serve: Slice steaks and drizzle sauce over the top.

Herb-Crusted Ribeye with Potato Gratin

Ingredients:

- 2 ribeye steaks (8 oz each)
- 1 cup breadcrumbs
- 1/4 cup grated Parmesan cheese
- 2 tbsp fresh parsley, chopped
- 2 tbsp fresh rosemary, chopped
- 2 tbsp olive oil
- Salt and pepper to taste

Instructions:

1. Preheat Oven: Preheat oven to 375°F (190°C).
2. Prepare Herb Crust: In a bowl, mix breadcrumbs, Parmesan, parsley, rosemary, olive oil, salt, and pepper.
3. Sear Steaks: Season steaks with salt and pepper. Heat a skillet over high heat and sear steaks for 3-4 minutes per side.
4. Crust and Bake: Place steaks in a baking dish, top with herb mixture, and bake for 10-15 minutes for medium-rare.
5. Serve: Let rest for a few minutes before serving.

Steak with Honey-Mustard Glaze

Ingredients:

- 2 sirloin steaks (8 oz each)
- 1/4 cup honey
- 2 tbsp Dijon mustard
- Salt and pepper to taste
- 1 tbsp olive oil

Instructions:

1. Make Glaze: In a bowl, mix honey, Dijon mustard, salt, and pepper.
2. Cook Steaks: Heat olive oil in a skillet over medium-high heat. Season steaks with salt and pepper and cook for 4-5 minutes per side for medium-rare.
3. Glaze Steaks: Brush honey-mustard glaze on steaks during the last minute of cooking.
4. Serve: Let rest before slicing and serve with extra glaze.

Chimichurri Flank Steak with Quinoa Salad

Ingredients:

- 1 lb flank steak
- Salt and pepper to taste
- 1/4 cup olive oil
- 1/4 cup red wine vinegar
- 1 cup parsley, chopped
- 4 cloves garlic, minced
- 1 tsp red pepper flakes
- 1 cup quinoa, cooked

Instructions:

1. Make Chimichurri: In a bowl, whisk together olive oil, red wine vinegar, parsley, garlic, red pepper flakes, salt, and pepper.
2. Marinate Steak: Place flank steak in a resealable bag and pour chimichurri sauce over it. Marinate for at least 1 hour (up to overnight).
3. Cook Steak: Preheat grill to medium-high heat. Remove steak from marinade and grill for 4-5 minutes per side for medium-rare.
4. Serve: Slice steak and serve over a bed of cooked quinoa, drizzled with additional chimichurri.

Garlic Butter Steak Bites

Ingredients:

- 1 lb sirloin steak, cut into bite-sized pieces
- Salt and pepper to taste
- 4 tbsp butter
- 4 cloves garlic, minced
- 2 tbsp fresh parsley, chopped

Instructions:

1. Cook Steak Bites: Season steak pieces with salt and pepper. In a skillet, melt butter over medium-high heat. Add steak bites and cook for 3-4 minutes until browned.
2. Add Garlic: Stir in minced garlic and cook for an additional minute.
3. Serve: Remove from heat, sprinkle with parsley, and serve immediately.

Steak and Potato Skewers

Ingredients:

- 1 lb sirloin steak, cut into 1-inch cubes
- 2 large potatoes, cut into 1-inch cubes and parboiled
- 1 red bell pepper, cut into squares
- 1 green bell pepper, cut into squares
- 2 tbsp olive oil
- Salt and pepper to taste
- 1 tsp garlic powder
- 1 tsp paprika

Instructions:

1. Prepare Marinade: In a bowl, mix olive oil, salt, pepper, garlic powder, and paprika.
2. Skewer Ingredients: Thread steak cubes, parboiled potatoes, and bell peppers onto skewers.
3. Marinate: Brush skewers with marinade and let sit for 30 minutes.
4. Grill Skewers: Preheat grill to medium-high heat. Grill skewers for 10-12 minutes, turning occasionally, until steak is cooked to desired doneness and vegetables are tender.
5. Serve: Remove from skewers and serve warm.

Grilled Hanger Steak with Pesto

Ingredients:

- 1 lb hanger steak
- Salt and pepper to taste
- 1/2 cup pesto (store-bought or homemade)

Instructions:

1. Season Steak: Preheat grill to high heat. Season hanger steak with salt and pepper.
2. Grill Steak: Grill for 4-5 minutes per side for medium-rare. Remove from grill and let rest for 5 minutes.
3. Serve: Slice steak against the grain and serve drizzled with pesto.

Spicy Steak Stir-Fry

Ingredients:

- 1 lb flank steak, thinly sliced
- 2 tbsp soy sauce
- 1 tbsp sesame oil
- 1 tbsp chili paste (or to taste)
- 2 cups mixed vegetables (bell peppers, broccoli, snap peas)
- 2 cloves garlic, minced
- 1 tbsp ginger, minced

Instructions:

1. Marinate Steak: In a bowl, mix soy sauce, sesame oil, and chili paste. Add steak slices and marinate for 15-30 minutes.
2. Stir-Fry: Heat a large skillet or wok over high heat. Add marinated steak and cook for 2-3 minutes. Add garlic, ginger, and mixed vegetables, and stir-fry for an additional 5 minutes until vegetables are tender-crisp.
3. Serve: Serve hot over rice or noodles.

Herb-Butter Basted Steak

Ingredients:

- 2 ribeye steaks (8 oz each)
- Salt and pepper to taste
- 4 tbsp butter
- 2 cloves garlic, smashed
- Fresh herbs (rosemary, thyme, or parsley)

Instructions:

1. Season Steaks: Season ribeye steaks with salt and pepper.
2. Cook Steaks: Heat a skillet over medium-high heat. Add steaks and cook for 4-5 minutes per side for medium-rare.
3. Baste: In the last minute of cooking, add butter, garlic, and herbs to the skillet. Tilt the skillet and use a spoon to baste the steaks with the melted butter.
4. Serve: Let rest for a few minutes before slicing and serving.

Steak with Sautéed Mushrooms and Onions

Ingredients:

- 2 sirloin steaks (8 oz each)
- Salt and pepper to taste
- 1 cup mushrooms, sliced
- 1 large onion, sliced
- 2 tbsp olive oil
- 1 tbsp balsamic vinegar

Instructions:

1. Cook Steaks: Season steaks with salt and pepper. Heat 1 tbsp olive oil in a skillet over medium-high heat. Cook steaks for 4-5 minutes per side for medium-rare. Remove from skillet and let rest.
2. Sauté Vegetables: In the same skillet, add remaining olive oil, mushrooms, and onions. Cook until softened, about 5-7 minutes. Stir in balsamic vinegar.
3. Serve: Slice steaks and top with sautéed mushrooms and onions.

Grilled Vegetable and Steak Sandwich

Ingredients:

- 1 lb flank steak
- Salt and pepper to taste
- 1 zucchini, sliced
- 1 red bell pepper, sliced
- 1 onion, sliced
- 4 sandwich rolls
- 4 tbsp mayonnaise or aioli

Instructions:

1. Grill Steak: Preheat grill to high heat. Season flank steak with salt and pepper and grill for 4-5 minutes per side for medium-rare. Remove from grill and let rest.
2. Grill Vegetables: Toss vegetables in olive oil, salt, and pepper. Grill for 4-5 minutes until tender.
3. Assemble Sandwiches: Slice steak and place on sandwich rolls. Top with grilled vegetables and a spread of mayonnaise or aioli.

Honey Garlic Flank Steak

Ingredients:

- 1 lb flank steak
- 1/4 cup honey
- 1/4 cup soy sauce
- 3 cloves garlic, minced
- 1 tsp ground ginger
- Salt and pepper to taste

Instructions:

1. Marinate Steak: In a bowl, mix honey, soy sauce, garlic, ginger, salt, and pepper. Place flank steak in a resealable bag and pour marinade over it. Marinate for at least 1 hour (up to overnight).
2. Cook Steak: Preheat grill to medium-high heat. Remove steak from marinade and grill for 4-5 minutes per side for medium-rare.
3. Serve: Let rest before slicing against the grain and serving.

Smoked Steak with Chimichurri

Ingredients:

- 2 ribeye steaks (1 inch thick)
- Salt and pepper to taste
- 1 cup chimichurri sauce (store-bought or homemade)

Instructions:

1. Prepare the Smoker: Preheat your smoker to 225°F (107°C) using your choice of wood chips.
2. Season Steaks: Season the ribeye steaks generously with salt and pepper.
3. Smoke Steaks: Place the steaks in the smoker and smoke for about 1-1.5 hours, or until they reach your desired internal temperature.
4. Sear (Optional): For a nice crust, remove the steaks from the smoker and sear them on a hot grill for 1-2 minutes per side.
5. Serve: Let the steaks rest for a few minutes before slicing and serve with chimichurri sauce.

Sesame-Crusted Steak with Soy Glaze

Ingredients:

- 1 lb flank steak
- Salt and pepper to taste
- 1/4 cup soy sauce
- 1 tbsp sesame oil
- 1/2 cup sesame seeds

Instructions:

1. Marinate Steak: In a bowl, mix soy sauce and sesame oil. Marinate flank steak for at least 30 minutes.
2. Coat with Sesame Seeds: Remove the steak from the marinade and season with salt and pepper. Press sesame seeds onto both sides of the steak.
3. Cook Steak: Heat a skillet over medium-high heat. Cook the steak for 4-5 minutes per side for medium-rare.
4. Serve: Let rest for 5 minutes, then slice against the grain and serve.

Red Wine-Braised Beef Short Ribs

Ingredients:

- 4 beef short ribs
- Salt and pepper to taste
- 2 tbsp olive oil
- 1 onion, chopped
- 2 carrots, chopped
- 2 cups red wine
- 1 cup beef broth
- 2 cloves garlic, minced
- 1 sprig thyme

Instructions:

1. Season Ribs: Preheat oven to 300°F (150°C). Season short ribs with salt and pepper.
2. Sear Ribs: Heat olive oil in a Dutch oven over medium-high heat. Sear short ribs on all sides until browned. Remove from pot and set aside.
3. Sauté Vegetables: In the same pot, add onion and carrots. Sauté for 5 minutes. Add garlic and cook for another minute.
4. Braise Ribs: Add red wine, beef broth, and thyme. Return ribs to the pot. Cover and braise in the oven for 3 hours or until tender.
5. Serve: Serve short ribs with sauce spooned over the top.

Steak Salad with Avocado and Feta

Ingredients:

- 1 lb sirloin steak
- Salt and pepper to taste
- 6 cups mixed greens
- 1 avocado, diced
- 1/2 cup feta cheese, crumbled
- 1/4 cup olive oil
- 2 tbsp balsamic vinegar

Instructions:

1. Cook Steak: Season the sirloin steak with salt and pepper. Grill or sear for 4-5 minutes per side for medium-rare. Let rest before slicing.
2. Assemble Salad: In a large bowl, combine mixed greens, avocado, feta cheese, and sliced steak.
3. Dress Salad: Whisk together olive oil and balsamic vinegar. Drizzle over the salad and toss gently to combine.
4. Serve: Serve immediately.

Mexican Street Corn and Steak Bowl

Ingredients:

- 1 lb flank steak
- Salt and pepper to taste
- 2 cups cooked rice
- 1 cup corn kernels (grilled or canned)
- 1/2 cup cotija cheese
- 1/4 cup cilantro, chopped
- 1 lime, juiced
- Chili powder to taste

Instructions:

1. Cook Steak: Season flank steak with salt and pepper. Grill for 4-5 minutes per side for medium-rare. Let rest before slicing.
2. Prepare Corn: If using canned corn, drain and rinse. If grilling, grill corn until slightly charred.
3. Assemble Bowls: In a bowl, layer rice, sliced steak, corn, cotija cheese, and cilantro.
4. Season and Serve: Squeeze lime juice over the bowls and sprinkle with chili powder before serving.

Garlic Herb Butter Steak Sandwich

Ingredients:

- 2 sirloin steaks
- Salt and pepper to taste
- 1/4 cup butter, softened
- 2 cloves garlic, minced
- 1 tbsp fresh parsley, chopped
- 4 sandwich rolls

Instructions:

1. Prepare Garlic Butter: In a bowl, mix softened butter with minced garlic and parsley. Set aside.
2. Cook Steaks: Season steaks with salt and pepper. Grill or sear for 4-5 minutes per side for medium-rare. Let rest before slicing.
3. Toast Rolls: Cut sandwich rolls in half and toast them lightly on the grill or in a pan.
4. Assemble Sandwiches: Spread garlic herb butter on the rolls, layer with sliced steak, and serve.

Classic Steak and Kidney Pie

Ingredients:

- 1 lb beef steak, cubed
- 1/2 lb kidney, cleaned and chopped
- 1 onion, chopped
- 2 cups beef broth
- 1 tbsp Worcestershire sauce
- Salt and pepper to taste
- 2 sheets puff pastry
- 1 egg, beaten (for egg wash)

Instructions:

1. Cook Filling: In a large pot, brown beef and kidney over medium heat. Add onion and cook until soft. Stir in broth and Worcestershire sauce. Simmer for 1 hour. Season with salt and pepper.
2. Prepare Pastry: Preheat oven to 400°F (200°C). Roll out one sheet of puff pastry and line a pie dish. Pour in the filling.
3. Top Pie: Cover with the second sheet of pastry, seal the edges, and cut a small hole in the center. Brush with beaten egg.
4. Bake: Bake for 30-35 minutes or until golden brown. Serve hot.

Steak Pizzaiola

Ingredients:

- 2 lbs flank steak
- Salt and pepper to taste
- 2 tbsp olive oil
- 1 onion, sliced
- 3 cloves garlic, minced
- 1 can (28 oz) crushed tomatoes
- 1 tsp oregano
- 1/2 tsp red pepper flakes

Instructions:

1. Cook Steak: Season flank steak with salt and pepper. In a skillet, heat olive oil and sear the steak for 4-5 minutes on each side. Remove and set aside.
2. Sauté Vegetables: In the same skillet, add onion and garlic, and sauté until soft. Stir in crushed tomatoes, oregano, and red pepper flakes.
3. Simmer: Return steak to the skillet, cover, and simmer for 20-25 minutes until steak is tender.
4. Serve: Slice steak and serve with the sauce over pasta or crusty bread.

Printed in the USA
CPSIA information can be obtained
at www.ICGtesting.com
CBHW081548141024
15841CB00003B/27